THE
CHOW DOWN

Irresistible cereal snack
mix recipes the whole
family will enjoy

Lynn April

Halo
Publishing International

ISBN: 978-1-61244-363-8
Library of Congress Control Number: 2015906881

Printed in the United States of America

Halo ● ● ● ●
Publishing International
www.halopublishing.com

Published by Halo Publishing International
1100 NW Loop 410
Suite 700 - 176
San Antonio, Texas 78213
Toll Free 1-877-705-9647
Website: www.halopublishing.com
E-mail: contact@halopublishing.com

To my father, who gifted me with a love
for microscopic organisms,
To my mother, who gifted me with a love
for writing and proper grammar,
And to my husband, who makes me better and
always encourages my dreams.

BOOK INTRO

From April 2011 until January 2014, I ran an in-home custom cake baking and decorating business. I loved every second of it until I didn't love it anymore and decided I needed to call it quits. A few months later, I started writing Fresh April Flours, a blog where I could share my recipes. Since then, I have taken much pleasure in virtually baking with people all over the world, and in helping bakers of all ages find a happy place within that is covered in powdered sugar.

Nothing makes me happier than when someone trusts my opinion enough to ask me for "the best" recipe for something they would like to make. That's what you'll find in this book: my favorite varieties of the ever-popular puppy chow. The recipes I've developed are easy and come together quickly, and several of them are flexible in the way of ingredients. Because puppy chow is more of a snack mix, it's easy to cater any specific recipe to your liking by adding or removing ingredients you love or don't love, increasing or decreasing amounts, and using your favorite varieties of each ingredient I suggest.

My recipes are simply a guide to creative snacking. I want you to have fun with your puppy chow, maybe get your kids involved (they're really good at shaking the bag), and turn these treats into something innovative you can use for entertaining, gifting, or simply enjoying as a weekday night treat.

Follow along with me! I promise, this will be delicious.

Before we get started...

You probably have a few questions, and I'm doing my best here to read your mind before you even have a chance to ask them.

First of all, what's puppy chow?

Let's set the record straight, this is not a food for dogs. It is a food for humans. Puppy chow, in its original form, is rice or corn cereal + butter + chocolate + peanut butter + powdered sugar.

While this original recipe is a perfect snack, foodies and other creative cooks have made all kinds of variations on this theme. One of my favorites, Cake Batter Puppy Chow (pictured on the cover), is the very first recipe in this book. I initially shared that recipe on my blog, but I decided to put it in this book because:

1. It was the variation that got my creative puppy chow juices flowing,

2. The photos needed a facelift, and

3. Who doesn't love SPRINKLES?

Ok, so why do you love puppy chow so much?

Puppy chow has been one of my favorite snacks since I was a kid. I have distinct memories of standing in the kitchen with my mom shaking the bag of powdered sugar, anticipating that first crunchy, chocolatey, peanut buttery, powdered chunk of cereal. Whenever I saw a box of Chex® in the cabinet, I knew what was coming my way.

Not only that, but puppy chow comes together quickly and easily, travels well to parties, packages up nicely for gifts or favors, and, in most variations, lasts for several days. It's always a crowd pleaser and appeals to all ages! What's not to love?

Is there anything you should know before you dive right in?

First and foremost, I always use Chex® brand cereals. I have tried using generic brands to make puppy chow in the past, and they just do not hold up as well as the brand name.

Secondly, I cannot stress enough the importance of using quality chocolate when melting your coating. My preferred brands are Ghiardelli®, Baker's®, and Hershey's®, and I always use bar chocolate or melting wafers. Do not use chocolate chips as your melting chocolate, unless otherwise stated. There are stabilizers in chocolate chips that help them keep their shape in things like cookies, and these added ingredients make it difficult for them to melt smoothly. I also like to use candy melting wafers (I prefer Wilton® brand) which you can find at any craft store in the candy and cake baking aisle.

For recipes that call for flavored extracts, the extracts must be added to your chocolate before melting. When moisture is added to melted chocolate, it causes seizing, meaning the chocolate will go from smooth and liquid to hard and crumbly. Melting the chocolate with the extract already in place (and in the exact amounts specified) will help prevent seizing.

When combining the cereal and chocolate coating, use a light hand to distribute everything evenly so as not to break the cereal. I find it easiest to put everything in a very large bowl and, using a spatula, scooping cereal up from the bottom with the bowl at an angle. Also, be patient while stirring. The chocolate will stay warm for quite some time, so there is no need to rush.

I state in my recipes that you should use a large zip-top bag or container with a tight-fitting lid to shake your coated cereal and powdered sugar together. I prefer the container route. It's a little less scary!

Use a baking sheet lined with foil or parchment paper to let your puppy chow cool. Leaving it in the bag or container to cool can trap heat and moisture and make your puppy chow soggy. Keep your chow nice and crunchy.

Do you think you're ready to chow down? Let's get snacking!

CAKE BATTER PUPPY CHOW

This particular puppy chow flavor was one of the first recipes
I posted on my blog. For that reason, I felt it necessary
to include it in my cookbook (and on the cover!). It was
this twist that opened my eyes to my obsession with creating
fun and innovative flavors based on the classic.

Time: 5 minutes, plus cooling **Makes:** 5 cups

INGREDIENTS

- 4 and 1/2 cups (122g) Rice Chex® cereal
- 4 Tablespoons (58g) unsalted butter, cut into 8 slices
- 8 ounces (227g) white chocolate
- 1 teaspoon vanilla extract
- 1 teaspoon almond extract
- 2/3 cup (105g) sprinkles of your choice
- 1 cup (120g) powdered sugar

INSTRUCTIONS

1. Pour the cereal into a large bowl and set aside.
2. In a medium saucepan over low heat, melt the butter, white chocolate, almond extract and vanilla extract, stirring constantly until completely melted. Remove from heat.
3. Immediately pour melted mixture over cereal and stir gently to coat.
4. Pour cereal into a large zip-top bag or large container with a tight-fitting lid and add the sprinkles. Shake until all of the sprinkles are dispersed evenly.
5. Add the powdered sugar and shake again until everything is coated. Spread onto baking sheet lined with foil or parchment and allow to cool. Discard excess powder. Store in an airtight container at room temperature up to one week.

SNICKERDOODLE PUPPY CHOW

There's something so simple about a buttery snickerdoodle cookie. The combination of cinnamon and sugar gives it that signature melt-in-your-mouth flavor, and this puppy chow is no different. Crunchy, buttery, and packed with cinnamon and sugar.

Time: 5 minutes, plus cooling **Makes:** 5 cups

INGREDIENTS

- 4 and 1/2 cups (122g) Rice Chex® cereal
- 8 ounces (227g) white chocolate
- 2 Tablespoons (29g) unsalted butter, cut into 4 slices
- 1 teaspoon vanilla extract
- 2 and 1/2 teaspoons ground cinnamon
- 1/4 cup (50g) granulated sugar
- 1 cup (120g) powdered sugar

INSTRUCTIONS

1. Pour the cereal into a large bowl and set aside.
2. In a medium saucepan, combine white chocolate, butter, vanilla extract, and cinnamon. Heat on low, stirring constantly until completely melted. Remove from heat.
3. Immediately pour melted mixture over cereal and stir gently to coat.
4. Sprinkle granulated sugar onto coated cereal and stir again, gently, to distribute sugar evenly.
5. Pour cereal into a large zip-top bag or large container with a tight-fitting lid and add powdered sugar. Shake until everything is coated. Spread onto baking sheet lined with foil or parchment and allow to cool. Discard excess powder. Store in an airtight container at room temperature up to one week.

COOKIES & CREAM PUPPY CHOW

Cookies and cream are a match made in flavor heaven. In this version of puppy chow, we're working with both semi-sweet and white chocolates, and bringing the two together with everyone's favorite cookie. Lots of crunch, lots of cream— everything you would expect from a snack worthy of its name.

Time: 10 minutes, plus cooling **Makes:** 5 and 1/2 cups

INGREDIENTS

- 8 Oreo® cookies
- 4 and 1/2 cups (122g) Rice Chex® cereal, divided
- 1 cup (120g) powdered sugar, divided
- 4 ounces (114g) semi-sweet chocolate
- 4 ounces (114g) white chocolate

INSTRUCTIONS

1. Place Oreos® in a blender or food processor and crush into a fine crumb. Add half of the Oreos® to one large zip-top bag or large container with a tight-fitting lid, and the other half of the Oreos® into a second large zip-top bag or large container with a tight-fitting lid. Add 1/2 cup (60g) powdered sugar to each bag or container and set aside.

2. Split the cereal into two large bowls (about 2 and 1/4 cups or 61g in each bowl). One will be for the "cookies" puppy chow, and the other will be for the "cream" puppy chow. Set aside.

3. Working with the semi-sweet chocolate first, place the chocolate in a small microwave safe bowl. Heat in microwave for 20 seconds on HIGH, stir, and heat again as necessary in 20-second increments until completely melted. Immediately pour melted chocolate over one bowl of cereal and stir gently to coat. Pour the coated cereal into one of the reserved bags or containers and shake until everything is coated. Spread onto baking sheet lined with foil or parchment and allow to cool. Discard excess powder.

4. Repeat steps with white chocolate and second bowl of cereal. You may pour the "cream" puppy chow onto the same baking sheet as the "cookies" puppy chow to cool. Toss together before serving. Store in an airtight container at room temperature up to one week.

S'MORES PUPPY CHOW

"First, you take the graham. You stick the chocolate on the graham. Then, you roast the mallow. When the mallow's flaming, you stick it on the chocolate. Then you cover it with the other end. Then, you scarf. Kind of messy, but good."—Ham Porter explaining to Scotty Smalls what a s'more is in *The Sandlot* I couldn't have said it better myself. No fire required.

Time: 5 minutes, plus cooling **Makes:** 5 and 1/2 cups

INGREDIENTS

- 4 and 1/2 cups (186g) Golden Grahams® cereal
- 6 ounces (170g) semi-sweet chocolate
- 4 Tablespoons (24g) marshmallow creme/fluff
- 1 cup (120g) powdered sugar
- 1/2 cup marshmallow bits or 1 cup mini marshmallows

INSTRUCTIONS

1. Pour the cereal into a large bowl and set aside.
2. In a medium saucepan over low heat, melt the chocolate, stirring constantly until completely melted. Remove from heat and add the marshmallow creme/fluff, but stir only a few times (so the marshmallow creates swirls).
3. Immediately pour melted mixture over cereal and stir gently to coat (mixture will be thick).
4. Pour cereal into a large zip-top bag or large container with a tight-fitting lid and add powdered sugar. Shake until everything is coated. You may need to break up large chunks with your fingers. Add marshmallow bits, and shake again. Spread onto baking sheet lined with foil or parchment and allow to cool. Discard excess powder. Store in an airtight container at room temperature up to one week.

MAYAN PUPPY CHOW

With this flavor combination, you're in for a spicy treat! I created
this version of puppy chow with Mayan culinary traditions in
mind— smooth chocolate, bitter cinnamon, and zesty chili powder
come together to create a snack that is like no other in this
book. The perfect balance of heat and sweet. If you dare,
consider upping the chili powder!

Time: 5 minutes, plus cooling **Makes:** 5 cups

INGREDIENTS

- 4 and 1/2 cups (180g) Cinnamon Chex® cereal
- 4 ounces (114g) semi-sweet chocolate
- 3/4 teaspoon ground cinnamon
- 1/2 teaspoon chili powder (add up to 1 teaspoon if you really love heat!)
- 1 cup (120g) powdered sugar

INSTRUCTIONS

1. Pour the cereal into a large bowl and set aside.
2. In a small saucepan, combine chocolate, cinnamon, and chili powder. Heat on low, stirring constantly until completely melted. Remove from heat.
3. Immediately pour melted mixture over cereal and stir gently to coat.
4. Pour cereal into a large zip-top bag or large container with a tight-fitting lid and add powdered sugar. Shake until everything is coated. Spread onto baking sheet lined with foil or parchment and allow to cool. Discard excess powder. Store in an airtight container at room temperature up to one week.

PEANUT BUTTER BUTTERSCOTCH PUPPY CHOW

Peanuts and butterscotch go so well together. The creamy, nutty peanut butter complements the extra sweet, brown sugary butterscotch to bring you a sweet-and-salty variety of puppy chow, with an extra crunch of salted peanuts. My taste-testers and I agree: this is probably the favorite puppy chow recipe in this book!

Time: 5 minutes, plus cooling **Makes:** 6 cups

INGREDIENTS

- 4 and 1/2 cups (122g) Rice Chex® cereal
- 2/3 cup salted peanuts
- 1 and 1/4 cup (280g) butterscotch morsels
- 1/4 cup (64g) creamy peanut butter
- 1 cup (120g) powdered sugar

INSTRUCTIONS

1. Pour the cereal and peanuts into a large bowl. Toss to combine and set aside.
2. In a large saucepan over low heat, melt the butterscotch morsels and peanut butter, stirring constantly until completely melted. Remove from heat.
3. Immediately pour melted mixture over the cereal and stir gently to coat.
4. Pour cereal into a large zip-top bag or large container with a tight-fitting lid and add powdered sugar. Shake until everything is coated. Spread onto baking sheet lined with foil or parchment and allow to cool. Discard excess powder. Store in an airtight container at room temperature up to one week.

CHAI TEA PUPPY CHOW

Chai tea is a spicy blend of fennel seed, cardamom, cloves, cinnamon, and ginger. It is a supremely fragrant black tea, and when combined with hot milk and a little sugar, it becomes one killer beverage, and is one of my favorite cold weather treats.

Time: 5 minutes, plus cooling **Makes:** 5 cups

INGREDIENTS

- 4 and 1/2 cups (122g) Rice Chex® cereal
- 8 ounces (227g) white chocolate
- 1 teaspoon vanilla extract
- 1 teaspoon ground cinnamon
- 1/2 teaspoon ground ginger
- 1/4 teaspoon cardamom
- 1 chai tea bag
- 1 cup (120g) powdered sugar

INSTRUCTIONS

1. Pour the cereal into a large bowl and set aside.
2. In a medium saucepan, combine white chocolate, vanilla extract, cinnamon, ginger, and cardamom. Empty contents of chai tea bag into saucepan. Heat on low, stirring constantly until completely melted. Remove from heat.
3. Immediately pour melted mixture over cereal and stir gently to coat.
4. Pour cereal into a large zip-top bag or large container with a tight-fitting lid and add powdered sugar. Shake until everything is coated. Spread onto baking sheet lined with foil or parchment and allow to cool. Discard excess powder. Store in an airtight container at room temperature up to one week.

Note: Cardamom can be expensive and/or hard to find. You may omit it. The cardamom in the chai tea bag will help bring the flavor to your puppy chow.

MOCHA PUPPY CHOW

Regular readers of my blog know my love for coffee runs deep. This puppy chow is an extension of that love and just another way to enjoy that coffee flavor outside of my morning cup. Is there coffee in the chocolate or chocolate in the coffee? You be the judge.

Time: 5 minutes, plus cooling **Makes:** 5 cups

INGREDIENTS

- 3/4 cup (90g) powdered sugar
- 1/4 cup (30g) unsweetened cocoa powder
- 4 and 1/2 cups (122g) Rice Chex® cereal
- 4 ounces (114g) semi-sweet chocolate
- 2 Tablespoons (10g) instant coffee granules

INSTRUCTIONS

1. In a large zip-top bag or large container with a tight-fitting lid, combine powdered sugar and unsweetened cocoa powder. Toss together and set aside.
2. Pour the cereal into a large bowl and set aside.
3. In a small saucepan, combine the chocolate and instant coffee granules, and melt over low heat until smooth. Remove from heat.
4. Immediately pour melted mixture over cereal and stir gently to coat.
5. Pour cereal into prepared bag or container and shake until everything is coated. Spread onto baking sheet lined with foil or parchment and allow to cool. Discard excess powder. Store in an airtight container at room temperature up to one week.

PIÑA COLADA PUPPY CHOW

It's completely acceptable to make piña colada-flavored anything any time of the year, in any season, while wearing flip flops and sunglasses. I would even fully support sticking a cocktail umbrella into this bowl of puppy chow. In fact… I insist. Bottoms up!

Time: 10 minutes, plus cooling **Makes:** 5 cups

INGREDIENTS

- 1/2 cup (60g) sweetened shredded coconut
- 1/4 cup pineapple-flavored gelatin mix (approximately half of a 3-ounce box)
- 1/4 cup (30g) powdered sugar
- 4 and 1/2 cups (122g) Rice Chex® cereal, divided
- 8 ounces (227g) white chocolate, divided

INSTRUCTIONS

1. In a food processor or powerful blender, pulse the shredded coconut into a fine powder. Pour the powder into a large zip-top bag or container with a tight-fitting lid. Set aside.
2. In a second large zip-top bag or large container with a tight-fitting lid, combine pineapple-flavored gelatin mix and powdered sugar. Toss together and set aside.
3. Split the cereal into two large bowls (about 2 and 1/4 cups or 61g in each bowl). One will be for the coconut puppy chow, and the other will be for the pineapple puppy chow. Set aside.
5. Place 4 ounces (114g) of the white chocolate in a small microwave safe bowl. Heat in microwave for 20 seconds on HIGH, stir, and heat again as necessary in 20-second increments until completely melted. Immediately pour melted chocolate over one bowl of cereal and stir gently to coat. Pour the coated cereal into the reserved bag or container of coconut powder and shake until everything is coated. Cereal will be sticky. Spread onto baking sheet lined with foil or parchment and allow to cool. Discard excess powder.
6. Repeat steps with remaining 4 ounces (114g) of white chocolate, second bowl of cereal, and reserved bag or container with pineapple-flavored gelatin mix. Because the coconut puppy chow is so sticky, spread pineapple puppy chow onto a separate baking sheet lined with foil or parchment. Combine both puppy chows before serving. Store in an airtight container at room temperature up to one week.

LEMONADE PUPPY CHOW

Nothing says summer more than a freshly squeezed glass of lemonade. It's my favorite part about the Jersey shore boardwalk (second to my vanilla cone with rainbow sprinkles). Crisp, tart, and sweet, all at the same time.

Time: 5 minutes, plus cooling **Makes:** 5 cups

INGREDIENTS

- 1/2 cup (60g) powdered sugar
- 1/2 cup (102g) powdered lemonade mix
- 4 and 1/2 cups (122g) Rice Chex® cereal
- 8 ounces (227g) white chocolate
- The zest of one lemon (approximately 2 teaspoons)

INSTRUCTIONS

1. In a large zip-top bag or large container with a tight-fitting lid, combine powdered sugar and powdered lemonade mix. Toss together and set aside.
2. Pour the cereal into a large bowl and set aside.
3. In a medium saucepan over low heat, melt the white chocolate and lemon zest, stirring constantly until completely melted. Remove from heat.
4. Immediately pour melted chocolate over cereal and stir gently to coat.
5. Pour cereal into prepared bag or container and shake until cereal is completely coated. Spread onto baking sheet lined with foil or parchment and allow to cool. Discard excess powder. Store in an airtight container at room temperature up to one week.

Note: Consider combining Lemonade Puppy Chow with Strawberries & Cream Puppy Chow (next page) to make Strawberry Lemonade Puppy Chow.

STRAWBERRIES & CREAM PUPPY CHOW

Juicy strawberries on top of a luscious bowl of sweetened cream…
It's a delightfully refreshing dessert. For an even better treat,
stick this puppy chow in the refrigerator.

Time: 5 minutes, plus cooling **Makes:** 5 cups

INGREDIENTS

- 1-3 ounce box strawberry-flavored gelatin mix
- 1/2 cup (60g) powdered sugar
- 4 and 1/2 cups (122g) Rice Chex® cereal
- 2 ounces (56g) cream cheese
- 6 ounces (170g) white chocolate

INSTRUCTIONS

1. In a large zip-top bag or large container with a tight-fitting lid, combine strawberry-flavored gelatin mix and powdered sugar. Toss together and set aside.
2. Pour the cereal into a large bowl and set aside.
3. In a medium saucepan, combine the cream cheese and white chocolate. Heat on low, stirring constantly until completely melted. Remove from heat.
4. Immediately pour melted mixture over cereal and stir gently to coat.
5. Pour cereal into prepared bag or container and shake until everything is coated. Spread onto baking sheet lined with foil or parchment and allow to cool. Discard excess powder. Store in an airtight container in the refrigerator up to 4 days.

Note: Consider combining Strawberries & Cream Puppy Chow with Lemonade Puppy Chow (previous page) to make Strawberry Lemonade Puppy Chow.

ORANGE CREAMSICLE PUPPY CHOW

Orange is one of my favorite flavors of anything, but when that bright, citrusy flavor is combined with smooth, creamy vanilla, the result is both sweet and tart. This puppy chow reminds me of popsicles in the summertime, dripping down my hand in the humid Pennsylvania air.

Time: 5 minutes, plus cooling **Makes:** 5 cups

INGREDIENTS

- 1-3 ounce box orange-flavored gelatin mix
- 1/2 cup (60g) powdered sugar
- 4 and 1/2 cups (180g) Vanilla Chex® cereal
- 8 ounces (227g) white chocolate

INSTRUCTIONS

1. In a large zip-top bag or large container with a tight-fitting lid, combine orange-flavored gelatin mix and powdered sugar. Toss together and set aside.
2. Pour the cereal into a large bowl and set aside.
3. Place the white chocolate in a small microwave safe bowl. Heat in microwave for 20 seconds on HIGH, stir, and heat again as necessary in 20-second increments until completely melted.
4. Immediately pour melted chocolate over cereal and stir gently to coat.
5. Pour cereal into prepared bag or container and shake until everything is coated. Spread onto baking sheet lined with foil or parchment and allow to cool. Discard excess powder. Store in an airtight container at room temperature up to one week. To make it feel more like a frozen treat, store it in the refrigerator.

NUTELLA® PUPPY CHOW

Let's face it— this puppy chow is really just an alternative to eating Nutella® right out of the jar (which I definitely would not judge you for doing). Chopped hazelnuts seal the deal and turn this otherwise smooth spread into an extra crunchy snack.

Time: 5 minutes, plus cooling **Makes:** 6 cups

INGREDIENTS

- 4 and 1/2 cups (122g) Rice Chex® cereal
- 2/3 cup coarsely chopped hazelnuts
- 3/4 cup (222g) Nutella®
- 4 ounces (114g) semi-sweet chocolate
- 1 cup (120g) powdered sugar

INSTRUCTIONS

1. Pour the cereal and hazelnuts into a large bowl and set aside.
2. In a medium saucepan, combine Nutella® and chocolate. Heat on low, stirring constantly until completely melted. Remove from heat.
3. Immediately pour melted mixture over cereal and nuts and stir gently to coat.
4. Pour cereal into a large zip-top bag or large container with a tight-fitting lid and add powdered sugar. Shake until cereal is completely coated. Spread onto baking sheet lined with foil or parchment and allow to cool. Discard excess powder. Store in an airtight container at room temperature up to one week.

BANANA BREAD PUPPY CHOW

Banana bread is one of those breads that just soothes the soul, and I created this flavor of puppy chow to do just that. Warm cinnamon and brown sugar notes accompany a punch of banana— all the flavor you would expect in banana bread, made extra crunchy with nuts and banana chips.

Prep time: 3 minutes **Total time:** 8 minutes, plus cooling **Makes:** 6 cups

INGREDIENTS

- 1-3.4 ounce package instant banana or banana cream pie pudding
- 1/4 cup (50g) brown sugar, loosely packed
- 4 and 1/2 cups (180g) Cinnamon Chex® cereal
- 8 ounces (227g) white chocolate
- 1 teaspoon vanilla extract
- 1 teaspoon ground cinnamon
- 1 and 1/2 ounces (40g) dried banana chips
- 1/2 cup coarsely chopped nuts of your choice (optional)

INSTRUCTIONS

1. Pour the instant banana pudding and brown sugar into a large zip-top bag or large container with tight-fitting lid. Toss together. Set aside.
2. Pour the cereal into a large bowl and set aside.
3. In a medium saucepan, combine white chocolate, vanilla extract, and cinnamon. Heat on low, stirring constantly until completely melted. Remove from heat.
4. Immediately pour melted mixture over cereal and stir gently to coat.
5. Pour cereal into prepared bag or container and shake until everything is coated. Spread onto baking sheet lined with foil or parchment and allow to cool. Discard excess powder. Add banana chips. Store in an airtight container at room temperature up to one week.

TIRAMISU PUPPY CHOW

This classic Italian dessert is the perfect marriage of several strong flavors. A combination of bitter semi-sweet chocolate and creamy white chocolate meets the sharp taste of coffee and the smooth flavor of rum. A coating of cocoa powder offers each bite of this puppy chow a tart exterior which gives way to a sweet and flavorful interior.

Time: 5 minutes, plus cooling **Makes:** 5 cups

INGREDIENTS

- 1/2 cup (60g) powdered sugar
- 1/2 cup (60g) unsweetened cocoa powder
- 4 and 1/2 cups (122g) Rice Chex® cereal
- 4 ounces (114g) semi-sweet chocolate
- 4 ounces (114g) white chocolate
- 1 and 1/2 teaspoons rum extract
- 2 and 1/2 Tablespoons (13g) instant coffee granules

INSTRUCTIONS

1. In a large zip-top bag or large container with a tight-fitting lid, combine powdered sugar and unsweetened cocoa powder. Toss together and set aside.
2. Pour the cereal into a large bowl and set aside.
3. In a medium saucepan, combine the semi-sweet chocolate, white chocolate, rum extract, and instant coffee granules. Melt over low heat until smooth. Remove from heat.
4. Immediately pour melted mixture over cereal and stir gently to coat.
5. Pour cereal into prepared bag or container and shake until everything is coated. Spread onto baking sheet lined with foil or parchment and allow to cool. Discard excess powder. Store in an airtight container at room temperature up to one week.

CORDIAL CHERRY PUPPY CHOW

Cordial cherries are just oozing with sweet, sticky cherry goodness, and somewhere inside there is an actual cherry. Although there is nothing gooey about this puppy chow, it's hard not to love chocolate and cherries together, especially when you don't have to worry about making a sticky mess of your face.

Time: 10 minutes, plus cooling **Makes:** 6 cups

INGREDIENTS

- 1/2 cup (60g) powdered sugar, divided
- 1/4 cup (30g) unsweetened cocoa powder
- 1/4 cup cherry-flavored gelatin mix (approximately half of a 3-ounce box)
- 4 and 1/2 cups (122g) Rice Chex® cereal, divided
- 4 ounces (114g) semi-sweet chocolate
- 4 ounces (114g) white chocolate
- 1 cup dried cherries

INSTRUCTIONS

1. In a large zip-top bag or large container with a tight-fitting lid, combine 1/4 cup (30g) of the powdered sugar and the unsweetened cocoa powder. Toss together and set aside.
2. In a second large zip-top bag or large container with a tight-fitting lid, combine the remaining 1/4 cup (30g) of the powdered sugar and the cherry-flavored gelatin mix. Toss together and set aside.
3. Split the cereal into two large bowls (about 2 and 1/4 cups or 61g in each bowl). One will be for the chocolate puppy chow, and the other will be for the cherry puppy chow. Set aside.
4. Working with the semi-sweet chocolate first, place the chocolate in a small microwave safe bowl. Heat in microwave for 20 seconds on HIGH, stir, and heat again as necessary in 20-second increments until completely melted. Immediately pour melted chocolate over one bowl of cereal and stir gently to coat. Pour the coated cereal into the reserved bag or container of powdered sugar and unsweetened cocoa powder and shake until everything is coated. Spread onto baking sheet lined with foil or parchment and allow to cool. Discard excess powder.
5. Repeat steps with white chocolate, second bowl of cereal, and reserved bag or container of powdered sugar and cherry-flavored gelatin mix. You may cool both puppy chows together on the same baking sheet. Add dried cherries. Toss everything together before serving. Store in an airtight container at room temperature up to one week.

BUTTERFINGER® PUPPY CHOW

Butterfinger® takes the whole chocolate and peanut butter
relationship to one of my favorite places—
crispy peanut butter heaven (with that unmistakable
flaky center that just melts in your mouth).

Time: 5 minutes, plus cooling **Makes:** 6 cups

INGREDIENTS

- 4 and 1/2 cups (122g) Rice Chex® cereal
- 6 ounces (170g) semi-sweet chocolate
- 1/2 cup (128g) creamy peanut butter
- 1 cup chopped Butterfinger® bars (approximately 7 fun size bars)
- 1 cup (120g) powdered sugar

INSTRUCTIONS

1. Pour the cereal into a large bowl and set aside.
2. In a medium saucepan, combine the chocolate and peanut butter. Heat on low, stirring constantly until completely melted. Remove from heat.
3. Immediately pour melted mixture over cereal and stir gently to coat.
4. Pour cereal mixture into a large zip-top bag or large container with a tight-fitting lid and add powdered sugar. Shake until everything is coated. Add chopped Butterfinger® bars and shake again until combined. Spread onto baking sheet lined with foil or parchment and allow to cool. Discard excess powder. Store in an airtight container at room temperature up to one week.

SEA SALTED CARAMEL PUPPY CHOW

The only thing that makes creamy, buttery caramel better is a little bit of sea salt. This puppy chow showcases caramel's dense and chewy texture by creating a unique exterior around each piece of cereal. While the cereal stays crunchy, the outside melts in your mouth as you sink your teeth through its caramel coating made from scratch.

Time: 7 minutes, plus cooling **Makes:** 5 cups

INGREDIENTS

- 4 and 1/2 cups (122g) Rice Chex® cereal
- 4 Tablespoons (58g) unsalted butter
- 3/4 cup (150g) brown sugar
- 4 Tablespoons (60 mL) light corn syrup
- 1/2 teaspoon vanilla extract
- 1/2 teaspoon sea salt or other coarse salt (not table salt)
- 1/2 cup (60g) powdered sugar

INSTRUCTIONS

1. Pour the cereal into a large bowl and set aside.
2. In a medium saucepan, combine the butter, sugar, and corn syrup. Heat on medium until entire mixture is at a rolling boil. Remove from heat and stir in vanilla extract and sea salt.
3. Immediately pour melted mixture over cereal and stir gently to coat.
4. Pour cereal mixture into a large zip-top.bag or large container with a tight-fitting lid and add powdered sugar. Shake until everything is coated. Spread onto baking sheet lined with foil or parchment and allow to cool. Puppy chow will harden as it cools. Discard excess powder. Store in an airtight container at room temperature up to one week.

PEANUT BUTTER & JELLY PUPPY CHOW

PB&J— such a perfect combination that it needs no introduction.

Time: 10 minutes, plus cooling **Makes:** 5 cups

INGREDIENTS

- 3/4 cup (90g) powdered sugar, divided
- 1/4 cup gelatin mix in the "jelly" flavor of your choice (approximately half of a 3-ounce box)
- 4 and 1/2 cups (122g) Rice Chex® cereal, divided
- 1/2 cup (120g) + 2 Tablespoons (30g) peanut butter chips
- 2 Tablespoons (32g) creamy peanut butter
- 4 ounces (114g) white chocolate

INSTRUCTIONS

1. Add 1/2 cup (60g) of the powdered sugar to a large zip-top bag or large container with a tight-fitting lid. Set aside.
2. Add the remaining 1/4 cup (30g) of the powdered sugar and the fruit-flavored gelatin mix to a second large zip-top bag or large container with a tight-fitting lid. Toss together and set aside.
3. Split the cereal into two large bowls (about 2 and 1/4 cups or 61g in each bowl). One will be for the peanut butter puppy chow, and the other will be for the jelly puppy chow. Set aside.
5. In a large saucepan over low heat, melt the peanut butter chips and peanut butter, stirring constantly until completely melted. Remove from heat. Immediately pour melted mixture over one bowl of cereal and stir gently to coat. Pour the coated cereal into the reserved bag or container of powdered sugar and shake until everything is coated. Spread onto baking sheet lined with foil or parchment and allow to cool. Discard excess powder.
4. Repeat steps with white chocolate, second bowl of cereal, and reserved bag or container of powdered sugar and fruit-flavored gelatin mix. You may cool both puppy chows together on the same baking sheet. Toss everything together before serving. Store in an airtight container at room temperature up to one week.

FLUFFERNUTTER PUPPY CHOW

The fluffernutter sandwich is kind of like the sweeter cousin of a PB&J. Nutty peanut butter meets sticky sweet marshmallow creme to create the perfect combination of salty and sweet. No judgment from me if you pack some fluffernutter puppy chow in place of your sandwich in your next lunch.

Time: 5 minutes, plus cooling **Makes:** 6 cups

INGREDIENTS

- 4 and 1/2 cups (122g) Rice Chex® cereal
- 1 cup (240g) peanut butter chips
- 2 ounces (57g) white chocolate
- 1/4 cup (64g) creamy peanut butter
- 4 Tablespoons (24g) marshmallow creme/fluff
- 1 cup (120g) powdered sugar
- 1 cup mini marshmallows or 1/2 cup marshmallow bits

INSTRUCTIONS

1. Pour the cereal into a large bowl and set aside.
2. In a medium saucepan over low heat, melt the peanut butter chips, white chocolate, and peanut butter, stirring constantly until completely melted. Remove from heat and add the the marshmallow creme/fluff, but stir only a few times (so the marshmallow creates swirls).
3. Immediately pour melted mixture over cereal and stir gently to coat (mixture will be thick).
4. Pour cereal into a large zip-top bag or large container with a tight-fitting lid and add powdered sugar. Shake until everything is coated. You may need to break up large chunks with your fingers. Add mini marshmallows and shake again. Spread onto baking sheet lined with foil or parchment and allow to cool. Discard excess powder. Store in an airtight container at room temperature up to one week.

MINT CHOCOLATE PUPPY CHOW

Mint and chocolate are a great flavor pair, gracing goodies and delighting tastebuds at all times of the year from Valentine's Day to Christmas. If you're a mint chocolate lover, this is one puppy chow you will find hard to stop reaching for. The Andes® mints bring the perfect balance of mint and chocolate to this crunchy treat.

Time: 5 minutes, plus cooling **Makes:** 5 cups

INGREDIENTS
- 3/4 cup (90g) powdered sugar
- 1/2 cup (30g) unsweetened cocoa powder
- 4 and 1/2 cups (122g) Rice Chex® cereal
- 2-4.67 ounce (132g) boxes Andes® creme de menthe thins

INSTRUCTIONS
1. In a large zip-top bag or large container with a tight-fitting lid, combine powdered sugar and unsweetened cocoa powder. Toss together and set aside.
2. Pour the cereal into a large bowl and set aside.
3. Unwrap the Andes® mints and place them in a medium size microwave safe bowl. Heat in microwave for 20 seconds on HIGH, stir, and heat again as necessary in 20-second increments until completely melted.
4. Immediately pour melted mints over cereal and stir gently to coat.
5. Pour cereal into prepared bag or container and shake until everything is coated. Spread onto baking sheet lined with foil or parchment and allow to cool. Discard excess powder. Store in an airtight container at room temperature up to one week.

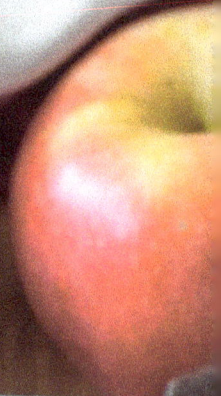

APPLE PIE PUPPY CHOW

My favorite pie is any kind with a streusel topping. In fact, I think streusel toppings belong on many things, which is why this puppy chow is not only spiced with the cinnamon and nutmeg flavors you love in apple pie, but it is also studded with homemade streusel bits and apple chips. It's like a slice of apple pie in each handful!

Prep time: 10 minutes **Total time:** 25 minutes, plus cooling **Makes:** 7 cups

Ingredients

STREUSEL

- 4 Tablespoons (58g) unsalted butter, cold and cut into 16 cubes
- 1/2 cup (100g) brown sugar, loosely packed
- 1/2 cup (40g) old-fashioned oats

CEREAL

- 4 and 1/2 cups (180g) Cinnamon Apple Chex® cereal
- 8 ounces (227g) white chocolate
- 2 Tablespoons (29g) unsalted butter, cut into 2 slices
- 1/2 teaspoon vanilla extract
- 1 teaspoon ground cinnamon
- 1/4 teaspoon ground nutmeg
- 1/4 teaspoon ground allspice
- 1 cup (120g) + 1/2 cup (60g) powdered sugar, divided
- 1 cup chopped apple chips or freeze-dried apples

Instructions

STREUSEL

1. Preheat oven to 350°F (175°C). Line a baking sheet with foil or parchment. Set aside.
2. In a small bowl, combine cubed butter, brown sugar, and oats. Press ingredients together with your fingers, creating chunks. Spread mixture onto prepared baking sheet and bake for 8-10 minutes, or until all the butter is melted. Mixture will spread over most of the baking sheet and will be soft. Remove from the oven and allow to cool completely on baking sheet. Streusel will harden as it cools.

CEREAL

1. Pour the cereal into a large bowl and set aside.
2. In a medium saucepan, combine white chocolate, butter, vanilla

extract, and spices. Heat on low, stirring constantly until completely melted. Mixture will be thick. Remove from heat.

3.   Immediately pour melted mixture over cereal and stir gently to coat. You may have to break up larger chunks with your hands.

4.   Pour cereal into a large zip-top bag or large container with a tight-fitting lid and add 1 cup (120g) of powdered sugar. Shake until cereal is completely coated.

5.   With your hands, break up the cooled streusel, add it to the cereal, and add remaining 1/2 cup (60g) of powdered sugar. Shake again until distributed. Spread onto baking sheet lined with foil or parchment and allow to cool. Discard excess powder. Add apple chips. Store in an airtight container at room temperature up to one week.

www.ingramcontent.com/pod-product-compliance
Lightning Source LLC
Chambersburg PA
CBHW041719090426
42739CB00018B/3477